The strange but true history of an unusual turn
of events at Boston's Charles Street Jail

PATRICK S. HALLEY
ILLUSTRATIONS BY BRENDAN TOTTEN

Bartow Books, 2015
Design by Adele Pollis and Rich Chiarella, AP Associates

Patrick S. Halley

Patrick S. Halley spent nine years doing advance work for Hillary Rodham Clinton. He was executive director of the Massachusetts Democratic Party and worked as an advance man or state director in six presidential campaigns. Prior to that he had a career in law enforcement, and served as chief of operations for both the Attorney General of Massachusetts and the Middlesex County District Attorney.

He resides in Florida and Massachusetts.

Other books by Patrick S. Halley

On the Road with Hillary, (Viking, 2002)

Wimpy, (Kelly Press, 2008)

Guide Dogs of America, A History, (Kelly Press, 2012)

Dapper Dan, America's Most Corrupt Politician, (Bartow Books, 2015)

Brendan Totten

Brendan Totten is an illustrator and print maker based in Somerville, Massachusetts. He studied at the School of the Museum of Fine Arts in Boston, and has done work for *Antcrank, Square Zeros, and The Huntington News.*

For Steve Graham, brother and partner in crime.

CONTENTS

ACKNOWLEDGEMENTS

I wish to thank John L. Ciardi for his significant contributions as editor and legal advisor to this work. His efforts made this a much better experience for the reader.

Also, Dr. Maurice Cunningham, friend and sage advisor, lent his knowledge of the Boston political scene and his formidable writing skills, and Kevin Saba contributed his unparalleled business acumen.

Steve Graham hovered over the project, encouraging, demanding, and critiquing at every step of the process. His contributions were invaluable.

I also wish to extend my gratitude to illustrator Brendan Totten, who's artwork brought the jail to life in a way that words alone could never accomplish, Adele Pollis and Rich Chiarella for their brilliant design work and Glenn Totten for lending his skilled professional eye.

LUXURY LOCKUP

The strange but true history of an unusual turn
of events at Boston's Charles Street Jail

THE
JOINT

Check out any travel guide to Boston, and you'll find the Liberty Hotel listed as one of the best, most luxurious places the city has to offer.

From the roof of the hotel, on the banks of the Charles River in the heart of downtown Boston, you can see in one direction the State House, the stately mansions of Beacon Hill and the glittering glass towers of Boston's business district. Turn the other way and you'll be greeted by college rowers gliding their sleek sculls through the water with power and grace, and across the river, the domes of the Massachusetts Institute of Technology and Harvard University.

But before it became a four star luxury hotel, the joint was known as the Charles Street Jail.

The hoosegow.

The clink.

The slammer.

The calaboose.

The place where Boston's miscreants spent their durance vile.

Built in 1851, its Quincy granite façade has marked one edge of the city for more than a century.

It's on the National Register of Historic Places.

And for the shenanigans that happened there in the middle of the Twentieth Century, it ought also to be on the National Register of Hysterical Places, if such a list exists.

There's nothing even vaguely funny about the design of the place though. Boston's best architect of the day, Gridley James Fox Bryant, designed the building, working with the Reverend Louis Dwight, a prominent prison reformer.

They used what was known as the "Auburn Plan," an English attempt to house prisoners in a humane environment.

No doubt the good reverend was thrilled that the joint was built in the shape of a cross, with four wings extending out from a central rotunda, allowing jail keepers to segregate prisoners according to gender, length of sentence, or type of crime.

Its interior soared ninety feet to a cupola that lit the atrium, and along the wings where prisoners were housed, thirty arched windows each thirty three feet in height, provided illumination that designers called "four times greater than the light in any prison yet constructed."

Despite all the careful planning and design, workers managed to commit a spelling error in the granite cornerstone of the building. It's one thing to misspell the word "superintendent" on paper, but when you chisel "superintendant" into granite, you've made a mistake for the ages.

Prisoners served their time in 220 granite cells, each eight feet by ten feet, fronted by an iron gate.

The campus also featured an outdoor exercise yard, a kitchen, a laundry and an infirmary.

The Suffolk County Sheriff, as keeper of the jail, was provided a comfortable house on the grounds, with impressive rooms and features. He also had a household staff of trustees to cater to his every need.

Over the years, the old joint was a stopping off place for quite a few notables, including James Michael Curley, Boston's famously corrupt Mayor, who enjoyed two stays; anarchists Sacco and Vanzetti; African-American activist Malcolm X; women suffragists who tried to shout down President Wilson during a Boston visit; and prisoners of war captured from German U-Boats menacing Boston Harbor during World War II.

The perpetrators of the famous Brinks Robbery, at the time the largest heist in American history, were held there while on trial, as was professional killer Elmer "Trigger" Burke, known as the "Rembrandt of the rifle" for his artistry with a machine gun. Burke was sent to Boston to murder Joseph "Specs" O'Keefe, one of the Brinks robbers. Boston cops arrested him before he could finish the job and sent him to the Charles Street Jail for possession of a machine gun. O'Keefe, who was also wanted for murder in New York, definitely did not find the accommodations to his liking and engineered a spectacular jail break involving three gunmen who broke *into* the jail to spring him and a fast getaway car to outrun the cops.

As thought provoking as that roster of famous inhabitants may be, it's nothing compared to the brief but tumultuous period from 1939 to 1941, when Sheriff John Dowd turned the Charles Street Jail into a luxury hotel for criminals.

THE
PERP

Johnny Dowd was, at heart, a criminal.

He was a true rogue, but in Boston rogues were tolerated and even admired in some circles. The transition from brazen rogue to outright criminal was easy for Johnny because he was born with larceny in his heart.

He came into the world in 1896 in Roxbury, the very center of Boston's thriving Irish-Catholic political hot-house. The Irish were in the process of wresting political and financial control from the Brahmins who had ruled the city since the days of the Pilgrims and had taken to hanging "No Irish Need Apply" signs in their shop windows as a means of slowing the inevitable tide of progress for people they considered unwashed immigrants. Tensions ran high and insults were hurled from both sides of the ethnic divide, with the Brahmins terming police vans "Paddy Wagons," "Paddy" being a derogatory term for an Irishman, and the Irish returning the favor by dubbing one fashionable Brahmin neighborhood "Tory Row," a not so subtle jibe at where their loyalties had been during the American Revolution.

Young John F. Dowd was a hustler. Never one to spend much time conforming to society's norms, he quit school at age twelve. He later claimed he did so to support his mother, but then, Johnny Dowd would claim a lot of things.

In addition to the usual odd jobs available to kids his age, such as selling newspapers or making deliveries for local merchants, Johnny developed a specialty of collecting cash donations for charities.

Johnny always had raffle tickets in his back pocket, supposedly to benefit some worthy cause or other, but oddly enough, the "winners" never seemed to live in his neighborhood.

Those lucky folks came from some town far from his Roxbury turf. He was a master at collecting to help out families in need due to a death, a fire, or the loss of a breadwinner, but somehow the cash he offered up to the afflicted never seemed to match the generosity of those who gave their contributions to young Johnny.

Boston politics in those days was a rough contact sport, and Johnny Dowd, a man of the streets known in every bookie joint, bowling alley and pool hall in the district, was soon on the varsity team. He hung out in the local ward room and polished his speaking skills delivering stem-winding speeches at street corner rallies to support the local democracy. Johnny was an "idea man" with a natural talent for spotting the next big con.

Politics gave him a wonderful opportunity to refine a scheme he would use throughout his career, the "Christmas basket." Throughout the year, the sharp dressed Johnny Dowd with the silver tongue would present himself on the doorstep of local merchants to request cash donations to be used to purchase turkeys, canned goods and other food staples for distribution to the neighborhood's poor families at Christmas time. Naturally, there was a mark up to cover overhead and expenses, which in Johnny's case amounted to the lion's share of what he wheedled out of the honest business people in his district.

Johnny's political rise was interrupted when he had to serve eighteen months in the Army in World War I. Although he managed to become a

Second Lieutenant in the Motor Transport Corps, he never saw any combat. He stuck with the Army Reserve after the war, becoming a First Lieutenant in the Quartermaster Corps, a position of bountiful opportunities for a man with such sticky fingers. Even in the Army during the war, Johnny's first thought was of self-promotion and pilfering.

Back on the home front, it was important that Johnny keep up the appearance of a legitimate businessman while he pursued his various illicit schemes. Like Chicago mobster Dean O'Banion, Johnny Dowd operated a floral shop as his visible source of income. Dowd's shop, on Warren Avenue, catered to the usual wedding and funeral trade, and also sold floral arrangements to the city for celebrations at an obscenely inflated price.

James Michael Curley, who would serve four terms as Boston Mayor, two terms as a Congressman, one term as Governor of Massachusetts and two terms in the Charles Street Jail, was the predominant power in the neighborhood, and Johnny signed up for his team.

Although Johnny Dowd never grew beyond five feet, four inches in height, and weighed in at a stocky one hundred and seventy pounds, with a nasty scar running down the right side of his face to his neck, he made up with oratory what he lacked in physical beauty. He used his skill at political speechmaking on Curley's behalf, echoing the rags to riches, up from the bootstraps, us-versus-them rhetoric that Curley perfected to woo Irish working class voters.

When Curley was elected Mayor, he rewarded Johnny by appointing him Director of Americanization[1] for the city, a position that was supposedly to educate the immigrant class in the finer points of citizenship, including of course, voting Democratic from the moment they qualified as a citizen.

---

[1] "Americanization" was vitally important because the World War had required millions of soldiers, including non-English speaking immigrants to volunteer for military service. The Department of the Interior held Americanization Conferences and called for active "reconditioning" of the poor and working class. An official Federal Government document of the day referred to what it termed the "alien problem" extant in 2,500 American cities, and urged local officials to take steps to assure that those aliens would respond to a military draft. Luckily, Johnny had passed the baton of leadership by the time they were needed to fight World War II.

After only eight months on the job, Johnny managed to move up to Curley's inner circle, becoming a member of the Secretariat, a position that allowed him to sell "protection" to his myriad collection of street thugs, bootleggers, bookies, and small time thieves. More often than not, that protection failed to keep the neer'-do-wells out of the slammer, causing Johnny to wring his hands, pout, and claim he was being double crossed by some crooked cop or other who refused to stay bought.

By the time he turned thirty, Dowd had his heart set on holding elective office. Why play the role of middleman when he could open his own franchise? He decided to run for the City Council. Curley had taken Johnny's measure and knew a hustler and sharpie when he saw one. He figured that not only would Johnny now be pocketing all the pelf he had been collecting and kicking up to Curley, he'd be a ticking time bomb likely to draw the attention of law enforcement at any moment. Curley demanded Dowd's resignation and supported his opponent in the City Council race.

Despite Curley's attempted roadblock, Johnny Dowd was elected to the Boston City Council in 1926, as a *reformer.* He spent more than $8,000 on his campaign, an amazing sum when one considers that the pay for a councilor was a mere $38.38 per week.

As a member of the City Council, Johnny talked a good game, even if his actions told another story entirely. He lit into the Boston Finance Commission, the city's fiscal watchdog agency for not being aggressive enough ferreting out corruption in the administration of Republican mayor Malcolm Nichols.

"The Fin Com is laying dead!" the bombastic Dowd screamed on the floor of the council. "This is in sharp contrast to what they did when Mayor Curley was in office!"

Meanwhile, the District Attorney assigned four full time detectives to look into graft among the council members. In August of 1927, Johnny Dowd was hauled before a Grand Jury to explain his role in awarding snow removal contracts. He had been a City Councilor for only eight months and he was already knee deep in fraud.

Two years later he was at the center of a fantastic scandal involving the Boston Braves baseball team. Boston's infamously strict "Blue Laws," dating to the time of the Puritans, restricted businesses from operating on Sundays. This was a major problem for big league baseball, since even if the games could be played, the team couldn't sell peanuts or crackerjacks to hungry fans. Late one night a member of the City Council cornered Judge Emil Fuchs, president of the Braves, in a downtown hotel and demanded he produce $5,000 bribes to each of thirteen of the councilors in return for their vote to lift the Sunday restrictions. Naturally, the larcenous Johnny Dowd was prominent among the dirty thirteen. In testimony before the Finance Commission about the attempted hold-up, Fuchs bristled at the fact that Johnny Dowd had also demanded a sizeable contribution from the team to the Roxbury Christmas Basket Fund, a cherry on top of the $5,000 bribe he wanted for his vote on the Sunday ordinance. Unfortunately for Johnny, all the public attention Judge Fuchs called to the attempted extortion shamed the city council into voting the right way without the benefit of cash payments to grease the wheels of bureaucracy. He did, however, manage to score a check for his infamous Christmas Basket Fund.

Johnny took a short break from his crooked council dealings to wed young Mary Margaret O'Connell of Dorchester. The councilor went big for his wedding, sending out two thousand invitations.

The wedding announcement said of the young groom:

"He is a past Grand Knight of the Rose Croix Council, Knights of Columbus; director of the Dudley Cooperative Bank; member of Bishop Cheverus Assembly; Fourth Degree, Knights of Columbus; the Alhambras; the Massachusetts Catholic Order of Foresters; and Roxbury Post of the American Legion."

The couple was wed at Saint Gregory's church in Dorchester on Monday, June 17th, 1929. More than 500 people attended a wedding breakfast at Rose Croix Hall in Roxbury, and newspapers reported the crowd at the church exceeded 1,500 people. Naturally, the more guests, the more wedding presents the councilor could expect. Best of all, since he got hitched on a Monday (it was Bunker Hill Day, a holiday peculiar to Boston celebrating a battle that actually took place on Breed's Hill), he was able to get a sizeable discount on renting the facilities.

His bride was the quintessential young Boston Irish-Catholic lass, except for one major shortcoming: she was a New York Yankees fan. It was a flaw that would come back to haunt Johnny Dowd many years later.

THE
TAKEOVER

With a new wife to support, Johnny Dowd began looking around for bigger opportunities to add to his treasure chest of graft. His eyes settled on the office of Sheriff of Suffolk County, the keeper of the Charles Street Jail.

In Massachusetts, sheriffs wield very little power in the law enforcement community, yet they enjoy enormous opportunities for patronage and the influence that comes from overseeing a vast budget. Unlike other states where the sheriff is the chief law enforcement officer, in the Bay State almost every community has a local police department, and the State Police cover whatever jurisdictions remain. The sheriff is relegated to transporting prisoners and maintaining the county jail where prisoners awaiting trial are housed, and the county House of Correction, where those convicted but sentenced to less than two and a half years are incarcerated. At the time, Suffolk County combined both facilities at the Charles Street Jail.

John A. Keliher, the incumbent sheriff, and a Democrat, had held the office for fifteen years. He was a former state legislator and also served three terms as a Member of Congress. Keliher was well liked and was regarded as a fair, humane, jail keeper.

11

The 1932 race between Keliher, Dowd and two other candidates would be waged city-wide across Boston, and in the neighboring communities of Chelsea, Winthrop and Revere, which made up the balance of Suffolk County. Democrats outnumbered Republicans by an almost ten to one ratio, meaning that the winner of the Democratic Primary would almost certainly be elected in the fall. Sheriff Keliher, taking no chances, placed his name on both the Democratic and Republican ballots.

Johnny Dowd opened his campaign by announcing that he had sent out 25,000 letters to voters touting his candidacy, and that he had 100,000 pledge cards printed and ready for use.

Just as he had campaigned for the city council as a reformer, Dowd jumped on the progressive bandwagon claiming that: "The sheriff's office can and should be conducted more economically." Dowd railed against Keliher, claiming "By refusing to purchase supplies for Charles Street Jail on a competitive basis, Sheriff John A. Keliher has deprived the taxpayers of Boston of thousands of dollars that could have been saved in feeding the prisoners." Ironically, if Johnny knew anything, it was how to deprive taxpayers of their money.

Taking to the airwaves of Boston's most influential radio station, the diminutive would-be lawman spoke of his council career in the third person: "Councilor Dowd," he said, "started and led the fight against street widening. Dowd opposed and voted against the last two municipal budgets, including the budgets of the Sheriff of Suffolk County."

Out on the streets, Dowd's rhetoric was much more inflammatory, and in at least one case led to bloodshed at a political rally. On the eve of the primary, more than 6,000 people jammed into Dudley Square, a crossroads in his home district of Roxbury named for a Colonial Governor of Massachusetts, to hear their native son explain how he would be the best thing since Sheriff Wyatt Earp. The weather was unseasonably warm, and the temperature of the crowd was decidedly hot. Shortly before the speaking program began, a would-be heckler was attacked by Dowd supporters and beaten so badly he had to be carted off to the hospital. With Johnny's street forces now fully fueled by alcohol and adrenaline, several more fistfights broke out, and police had to be

rushed to the scene from a nearby precinct house. Dowd was forced to stop mid-speech to allow the cops to quell a mini-riot.

When the votes were counted the next night, Johnny Dowd went down to defeat.

He had spent lavishly on his campaign and ended up with a fistful of unpaid bills for posters, campaign headquarters, and various other expenses associated with his attempt to move up the political food chain.

Being the scoundrel he was, Johnny steadfastly refused to pay up. Creditors hounded him night and day, and eventually dragged him into court where he claimed bankruptcy. It was a move he was quite familiar with, having resorted to the ploy three times in the past when the bills came due for his elaborate expenditures as a city councilor. He was such a familiar face in debtor's court that he was on a first name basis with the clerks there.

Johnny limped back to City Hall and resumed his undistinguished career as a city legislator, but he never lost the hunger for the power and prestige of the sheriff's office and its three and a half million dollar budget. When the office came up for election again in 1938, Johnny was the first in line to take out nomination papers to give it another shot.

Because the county was so lopsidedly Democratic, the Republicans didn't even bother to field a legitimate candidate. Keliher put his name on both the Democratic and Republican ballots as he had done in each of the past four elections.

The sheriff, now aged seventy one, was in failing health. Dowd attacked him mercilessly on the campaign trail, claiming Keliher was unable to perform the basic duties of the office and that he was only running because he was instructed to do so by the political bosses of the county.

Keliher countered by accusing Johnny of selling Works Progress Administration jobs to welfare recipients in the county, and pointing out that the sticky fingered councilor was under investigation for pocketing missing welfare checks. Like his Christmas basket racket, Johnny always had his fingers in the collection plate when public funds were being distributed.

It was cold, dark, and rainy on Election Day, and Dowd's troops splashed through the gloom delivering voters to the polls. Keliher was in no shape to counter the move and watched helplessly as carload after carload of Dowd loyalists were deposited at the polling places.

After the polls closed Johnny and his supporters gathered at a local hotel to anxiously await the outcome. Early returns showed that their effort at getting out the vote had paid dividends: it was becoming increasingly clear that John F. Dowd would be the new High Sheriff of Suffolk County.

Over at the Charles Street Jail, the mood in the sheriff's residence was anything but joyful. As precinct after precinct reported their votes for Johnny Dowd, Sheriff Keliher become more and more agitated. His campaign handlers urged him to calm down, but Sheriff Keliher was not a man to take defeat lightly. Shortly before the returns became final, Sheriff Keliher had a heart attack, collapsed, and died.

Johnny Dowd was declared the Democratic nominee, and his opponent in the fall election would be the recently deceased John A. Keliher.

Massachusetts law provides that in the case of a vacancy in the office of sheriff, the Governor can appoint someone to serve until the next election. The Governor at the time was Charles "Chowder Head" Hurley, widely regarded as one of the worst governors in the history of the state. Chowder Head took little time in appointing Johnny Dowd, his kindred spirit, as sheriff, and Dowd was sworn into office on October 5, 1938, taking over a three and a half million dollar budget.

The people of Suffolk County were about to witness something unique in the history of law enforcement.

THE BEST LITTLE JAILHOUSE IN AMERICA

You can't make this stuff up.

Johnny Dowd's run as sheriff began with a testimonial dinner in the Grand Ballroom of the Copley Plaza Hotel, one of the fanciest function halls in the city. All the swells were there: Governor Leverett Saltonstall, the horse-faced Yankee reformer, Attorney General Paul A. Dever, and the Honorable John P. Higgins, Chief Justice of the State Supreme Judicial Court. It was a white-tie event, with fifteen hundred paying guests. The testimonial committee presented Mrs. Dowd with a handsome watch, and then grandly presented the High Sheriff with the keys to a shiny new automobile, the $2,500 price tag of which included a $450 cash kick-back to Johnny.

Governor Saltonstall lauded the new lawman: "I know the new sheriff is going to serve a great many years, honorably, and with dignity and in humane, courageous fashion."

(The governor would indeed soon see Johnny serving many years…as a prisoner.) "We have seen Sheriff Dowd serve in the office for a month," the Chief Justice enthused, "we have had a new lease on life, as far as cleanliness and discipline are concerned." (True, the sheriff was *very* disciplined at

cleaning out the last vestiges of normalcy from the jail.)

Johnny Dowd then rose to complete the farcical entertainment that would prove to be the mirror image of reality.

"In the sheriff's office there is patronage," Johnny intoned with a sense of annoyance, "Well meaning friends come to me for favors for deserving persons. There never will be a man who tries to buy a job placed on the payrolls of the county as long as I am sheriff!"

The lights were barely out in the ballroom before Johnny announced to each of his 200 employees that they did indeed have to buy their jobs from him, or face immediate termination. The prices varied according to the job, with even the poor scrub women having to pay in cash. The going rate for a prison guard was more than a year's salary. Guards who wanted to stay on the job had to raid their savings accounts or take out sizeable loans.

Johnny placed three of his relatives, his sister, an aunt, and his wife's aunt on the payroll in jobs that had no defined duties.

When some of the guards balked at the exorbitant extortion, they were summarily dismissed onto the depression era streets and their jobs were sold to newcomers. One poor soul had worked at the jail for twenty-two years, and when he refused to pay he got the heave-ho. He ended up in an insane asylum within a week. In the first month of his administration Johnny axed men who had been with the department for ten, twenty or more years if they didn't pony up the cash.

The base pay for the sheriff was $4,000 per year. Deputies were paid somewhat less, but supplemented their income by being paid to serve legal summonses, a quirk in the Massachusetts judicial system that persists to this day. The funds from those process servers was placed in a pool and distributed evenly among all deputies once a month.

Johnny immediately filed a bill at city hall to double his own salary to $8,000 per year, and then announced to the deputies that, unlike other sheriffs, he would be taking $500 per month off the top of their process server's pool. Needless to say, the morale of the employees of the Suffolk Sheriff's Office nosedived immediately. They had no idea how bad things were about to get.

Sheriff Keliher had managed to live quite comfortably in the residence at the jail for nearly two decades. It was a nice house, with a view of the Charles River, a formal entryway and a wood paneled dining room. Johnny wasn't satisfied with the house or the perks that came with the job, such as a cook, maids, trustees to shine his shoes, tend his garden and drive his limousine. No, nothing but the best would do for him now that the taxpayers were footing the bill. He immediately set out on a full scale renovation of the residence which included new carpets, drapes, dinnerware, and the installation of a "whoopee bar" in the basement. The cost for new furniture was so exorbitant that sales people at the furniture company wondered how he would fit all the items in the house. That wouldn't be a problem for Johnny because it so happened that a substantial part of the new furniture would be used at his privately owned summer home on Cape Cod.

In the jail proper, to use that term loosely, Johnny Dowd was about to pioneer a new concept in jail management: concierge service for prisoners.

Johnny Dowd's jail was a pay as you go operation. For a reasonable fee, any prisoner could have his cell door unlocked twenty four –seven, and was free to wander about the joint at will. Henceforth, there would be no such thing as set visiting hours, prisoners could greet guests anytime they wished. The door separating the male and female wings of the jail was unlocked, and paying prisoners could enjoy conjugal visits in their bunks.

Johnny recruited prisoner William Forgrave, formerly president of Boston's Anti-Saloon League, to be the in-house bookie. Prisoners could place bets on sporting events or horse races, and Johnny sold them tip sheets and the Racing Form.

An area of the jail's infirmary was turned into a casino, with table games including blackjack, roulette, and dice, and yet another area was dedicated to a never ending high stakes poker game.

Guards were ordered to cater to prisoners desires, and were treated like uniformed waiters and busboys. Prisoners could order drinks from a service bar to be served to them in their cell, or drugs from the infirmary. When one poor guard balked at administering a drug that a prisoner had bought, Sheriff Dowd personally stormed into the cell, berated the cringing guard for his insubordination, and stood by while the chastened staff member gave the prisoner his drug.

Naturally, a high end restaurant was necessary to compliment the other enhancements Johnny was making to *"the prison experience,"* and so he opened one. Steak, lobsters, and Italian delicacies were cooked to perfection and served on formal dinnerware. Prisoners were encouraged to patronize the facility and to invite their friends to join them after Boston's legitimate bars and restaurants closed for the night. There was never a closing time at Johnny's jail. The outsiders gave some pizzazz to the place, and they were big spenders and good tippers. Johnny, of course, insisted that the guards turn over all tips to him. If the fare at Johnny's restaurant wasn't to their liking, prisoners were invited to call for delivery service from local establishments. (I told you, you just can't make this stuff up.)

One night a large champagne party got particularly boisterous with prisoners and guests swilling alcohol, singing bawdy songs and dancing a conga line through the cellblocks. As dawn approached one of the female guests well into her cups got an idea. "Let's go wake Johnny up and tickle his toes!" Why should the sheriff miss out on such a swell party at his own jail?

Prisoners had free access to the telephone, and one enterprising inmate ran his insurance business from the jail, hiring other prisoners to serve as clerks, and meeting clients in the jail's visiting room.

Johnny regularly berated the guards in front of the prisoners, screaming at one man who had displeased him by disciplining a prisoner for misbehaving: "Mind your own business, or have your buttons torn off!"

More disturbing, the prisoners also had access to the jail's armory, assuring that they would be better armed than the guards if there were ever a confrontation. Not that there was much chance of a confrontation, the prisoners had it made. Some were even allowed to call a taxi to take them to play golf at the nearby Fresh Pond Golf course.

On days they couldn't get a tee time, some prisoners practiced their game in the jail's courtyard. One afternoon a minister was in the jail's chapel performing a shotgun wedding. The chapel was filled with flowers, organ music and men in prison uniforms. Just as the clergyman was about to

administer the vows, one of the chapel's stained glass windows was shattered and a golf ball rolled to his feet. Turns out one of the golfing prisoners was having a hard time controlling his slice.

Another prisoner, doing time for political corruption, asked Johnny for permission to leave the jail to attend the noontime funeral of a friend and fellow politician from a neighboring city. Johnny readily consented, provided that the man would pay to take a deputy with him for appearances sake. He did so and set off for the funeral. Hours and hours passed, and there was no sight of the prisoner or the guard. Supper time came and went, and the lights were turned on, and yet the prisoner and the guard still did not materialize. Even Johnny started to get a little worried. The last thing he wanted to do was sound the alarm about an escape, that would only bring unwelcomed scrutiny to the operation he was running. Finally, well after two o'clock in the morning, there was a knock at the jail's front door. The prisoner was standing there with a sheepish grin on his face, and the guard was passed out drunk on the doorstep. "I've been trying to get this son of a bitch back here all day!" the prisoner moaned. "He wouldn't stop drinking. I'm tired and would really like to get back to my cell and get some rest."

The jail's fleet of cars became a limo service for favored prisoners, with trustees serving as chauffeurs. A female inmate alighted from the jail one bright morning and was mussing that she didn't know where to go that day. "What do you recommend?" She asked the trustee assigned to drive her. "Should we go to the beach or to the mountains?"

"Look, lady," the trustee responded, "It makes no difference to me. I've got a two year sentence, and a full tank of gas."

A comely female staffer who had caught Johnny's eye was picked up each morning at her Back Bay apartment and driven to "work" at the jail. After a long day of seeing to the Sheriff's every need, the limousine deposited her back home safe and sound.

One day Johnny looked out into the courtyard and realized that his own limousine was missing. Closer inspection offered no sight of the car or the trustee who had been polishing it an hour earlier. Hours passed, and the car and the inmate were still missing.

Just before dinnertime the car came gliding back into the lot with the trustee tipsy at the wheel and grinning from ear to ear.

"Where the hell have you been?" Johnny demanded of the man.

"You know, all that polish parched my throat something fierce." The trustee exclaimed. "I decided to duck downtown for a couple of cold beers to take the edge off."

"Well next time make sure you tell someone where you're going!" Johnny screamed at the man. "I almost had to use someone else's car to get to the racetrack."

During his campaign for office, Johnny had made a big deal out of the sheriff's purchasing policies. When he became sheriff, he instituted some extraordinary policies of his own. Despite the fact that cell doors were rarely if ever locked, Johnny had all of the locks replaced once a month because he was receiving a sizeable kickback from the locksmith. New water coolers were purchased for the jail at three times the market rate for similar devices. The butter contract was such a money maker for Johnny that prisoners were served a half pound of butter with every meal. Prices for every commodity used in the jail, from heating oil to food and even toilet paper were inflated and Johnny got a kickback.

Political corruption was nothing new in Boston, and it wasn't confined to the Charles Street Jail. Johnny, of course, was on a first name basis with most of the offenders from his days in City Hall, and he welcomed them with open arms to his cozy little jail.

J. Walter Quinn had been treasurer of James Michael Curley's campaign for governor, and to put it politely, not all of the money for that campaign was clean as the driven snow. Quinn had also hooked up with Emund L. Dolan, who was City Treasurer under Curley, and served as a front man so that Dolan could use taxpayer money to buy insurance bonds from the company Dolan owned with Quinn fronting as a "disinterested" owner. When they got caught the two decided the best way out was to fix the jury, but their ham handed attempts to do so only landed them in more hot water. Things got so bad that Dolan had to sell his 95 foot motor yacht, *The Maicaway* (a play on The Jamaica Way, the road where Curley's opulent and wildly controversial mansion was located…but that's a whole other story).

Quinn had already checked into his room at the Charles Street Jail by the time Dolan was dropped off in handcuffs. Johnny was waiting to greet him, and proudly ushered him through the establishment while explaining the ground rules.

"You'll find the service good here, even if I do say so." Johnny beamed. "Make yourself at home, Eddie. You're a hell of a fellow, and I like you. You're going to enjoy it here, but just to keep the record straight, so there'll be no misunderstanding, it's going to cost you about as much as a stay at the Ritz. You can stand that, can't you?"

Dolan, who was flush with cash from the sale of his yacht was only too happy to comply. "Sure, Johnny," the crooked city official nodded, "anything you say."

After a full tour of the facility Dolan settled on a nice private room in the infirmary where he would be close to his pal Quinn, and never too far away from the high stakes poker game where he hoped to win enough money to fund his stay.

Word soon started to spread among the criminal class: the Charles Street Jail was the place to be, the Best Little Jail House in America. That gave Johnny, ever the innovator, yet another amazing idea: why not rent out jail cells to criminals who were on the lam? The accommodations and extracurricular activities were first rate, and who would ever think of looking for fugitives in a jail?

Over the decades, Boston has had more than its share of rogues and frauds. Ponzi ran his scheme here and lives on in infamy. Johnny certainly deserves a prominent place in the pantheon of brazen hucksters. The idea of renting jail cells as a place for mobsters to hide, and charging them exorbitant rents was a DaVinci like stroke of the mastery of the fine art of fraud.

New York mobsters took Johnny up on the offer and rented a suite of rooms. They then used the jail laundry to start a scheme to make money. Unsuspecting customers dropped their laundry off at a non-descript storefront in downtown Boston, and it soon went out the back door into a van waiting to take it to the jail laundry where the city provided the soap,

water, machine and low paid prisoners to wash and fold. The clean clothes were delivered back to the storefront where customers paid up and were none the wiser. Johnny was only too happy to take his cut.

Another notable figure who rented space from Johnny was Edward J. "Easy Eddie" O'Hare from Chicago. O'Hare was the father of Butch O'Hare who would be awarded the Congressional Medal of Honor in World War II, and have one of the world's busiest airports named after him. He was also a confidant of mobster Al Capone, and had testified for the prosecution in the tax case that landed old Scar Face in prison. Easy Eddie ran dog tracks in Illinois and Taunton, Massachusetts, which is where he crossed paths with Johnny. By the time Johnny got his jail running to his satisfaction, Easy Eddie need a place to hide, not from the cops, but from Capone's button men who wanted to give him a Tommy Gun salute.

As Johnny prepared to celebrate his first year as sheriff, the Charles Street Jail had been transformed into a jail like no other, before or since. Give the man his due, he had the joint running like a well oiled machine, all but printing money, coming up with scheme after scheme, and he was quite proud of himself. However, he wouldn't have much time to rest on his laurels.

THE
JIG IS UP

Fall in New England is a beautiful time of year, with cool mornings, warm sunny afternoons and a kaleidoscope of colorful foliage. It should have been a triumphant backdrop for Johnny to celebrate his first anniversary as sheriff, but that was not to be the case. Instead, it would be the season of his downfall.

The chain of events that led to the end of Johnny's perfect little jail started months earlier just up the street at the Suffolk Superior Courthouse. Ruben Lurie, a young, hard charging attorney, happened upon two women crying in the back office of the Clerk of Courts. He inquired about the cause of their distress, and was shocked to learn that they had just been terminated from their jobs for refusing to pay to keep them.

The Clerk of Courts, like the Suffolk Sheriff, was an elected official, and taking a page from Johnny's playbook, he was demanding that his employees buy their jobs or hit the streets.

Lurie was outraged at this unethical conduct and acting on his own as a private attorney began gathering facts. Word spread around the courthouse that some sort of an investigation was underway and there was

27

broad speculation but no real hard information about what he was doing. The political hacks and grifters who habituated the courthouse hallways got nervous and their tongues started wagging.

The president of the Boston Bar Association, a powerful body that had recently caused the impeachment of two crooked District Attorneys, heard the rumblings and asked Lurie in for a meeting. When the young attorney told him what he was up to and shared some of the evidence he had gathered so far, the president invited him to act on behalf of the association and bring its full investigative weight to bear. Lurie jumped at the opportunity.

Operating now under the auspices of the Bar Association, which had been granted authority to pursue the matter by the Supreme Judicial Court of Massachusetts, Lurie summonsed each and every employee of the clerk's office in for a deposition. Time after time, under oath, he was informed of demands for money to be paid in cash if employees wanted to keep their jobs.

Lurie reported his findings back to the Bar Association, and they filed a petition before the Supreme Judicial Court to remove the clerk from office. So substantial was the evidence that Lurie compiled that the clerk surrendered immediately and resigned before he could be impeached.

Lurie, who would go on to have a distinguished career including stints as state Commissioner of Corrections and as a Superior Court justice, did not pause long to celebrate his triumph. He was bothered by something he had heard in the process of deposing the employees of the clerk's office.

"If you think things are bad in our office," one woman had testified, "you ought to drop around to the jail. They're much worse there. My cousin works in the boiler room and I know." Lurie took this new nugget of information to the president of the Bar Association, who immediately agreed that a full scale investigation was warranted.

Lurie was back in business, and Johnny's days were numbered.

Again using the offices of the Bar Association, Lurie began deposing the employees of the jail one by one. It didn't take long to realize that the woman from the clerk's office had been telling the truth. The stories Lurie heard about extorting money from employees for cash for their jobs was far worse than it had been at the clerk's office. Even more disturbing, Lurie started hearing details of the shenanigans at the jail: racketeers renting jail cells, prisoners running rampant, vendors of every sort being shaken down. He decided that he had a real can of worms to deal with at the jail.

Johnny got wind of the investigation and scrambled to try to cover his tracks. He announced that he was conducting his own investigation and would be *shocked* to learn that any man or woman had paid for their job. He called them into his office one by one and made it as clear as possible that there would be serious consequences for anyone cooperating with Lurie's probe.

Johnny was somewhat blind to the repercussions waiting for him. Although he was devious and cunning, he never seemed to think his schemes through to their likely consequences. He used heavy-handed tactics, bluff and bluster, and repeatedly failed to cover his tracks, launder his cash, or anticipate in advance what his opponents might do.

Two things that Johnny hadn't counted on would soon see him turning tail and running away. The first was the out and out hostility he had engendered among the guards and the other employees. They were hard working public servants who knew what a real jail looked like and how it ran, and they resented the criminal funhouse on the Charles that Johnny was running. The other hiccup that Johnny never saw coming was that some of the guards had made their cash payment to him with marked bills. Later protestations of innocence would be useless when the doctored cash was found in one of Johnny's safe deposit boxes.

As usual, the bombastic Johnny presented a false front to the media and the public. "This is a frame-up started by my political enemies," the sheriff proclaimed. "About ten days ago the press of Boston carried a report that the Boston Bar Association has appointed a committee to investigate the office of a certain Suffolk County official. At the time this story was published I paid little attention to it because I knew of no reason whatsoever why my department should be under the slightest investigation."

Meanwhile, Johnny did what all criminals do: he lawyer up.

The Bar Association went public with the results of their investigation and their petition to the Supreme Judicial Court to impeach Johnny. They charged: "Sheriff Dowd has been guilty since October 13, 1938, of malfeasance, misfeasance, nonfeasance in his office and has conducted himself in said office in an unlawful and reprehensible manner and is an unfit person to hold said office."

The Supreme Judicial Court immediately summonsed Dowd to appear before them to answer the charges. Dowd's attorney countered by claiming the Bar Association's charges were vague and asked for more particulars of what, exactly, the sheriff was being charged with doing.

The Bar Association fired back in court, sending Lothrop Withington, their top legal gun, to brief the justices. The tales Withington related about pay for jobs, criminals running the jail, vendors being extorted and the public purse being plundered so startled the members of the court that the Chief Justice asked somewhat incredulously if Withington was prepared to prove these fantastic charges. He was.

Meanwhile as the Bar Association's initial report circulated, the Internal Revenue Service and the District Attorney began their own investigations and proceedings against Johnny. He was now fighting losing battles on three fronts as the Feds began poking through his records and the Suffolk County Grand Jury began hearing testimony from those Johnny had swindled.

The Supreme Judicial Court scheduled its first session to consider Johnny's impeachment for Monday, November 13, 1939, and announced that Sheriff Dowd would be the first witness called. Rumors began circulating around the jail and the courthouse that Johnny would fall on his sword and resign rather than face a public inquisition. Johnny steadfastly denied the rumors and told one and all that he was looking forward to his day in court so that he could clear his good name. But Johnny was no fool when push came to shove. He realized that he could never beat the legal army lining up against him.

The weekend before he was scheduled to begin his defense, Johnny made the rounds of a few of his safe deposit boxes and quietly slipped out of Boston. By this time, the Suffolk County Grand Jury had handed up a secret indictment, and Boston being Boston, Johnny had gotten word of his impending arrest.

At 10:50 PM on Saturday night, November 11th, New York City Police were called to investigate reports of a man passed out on East 77th Street and bleeding profusely from his head. Officers from the 19th Precinct responded and found a thoroughly intoxicated man lying on the sidewalk, curled up in a ball and clutching his bleeding head. They helped the man to his feet and asked him who he was and what had happened. The man told the officers he was John F. Dowd, a florist from Boston, and that he couldn't recall what had led to his present condition.

A wagon was called and Johnny was brought to the precinct house on 67th Street to be booked into the drunk tank. As he was being processed, the police emptied his pockets and were astonished to find six thousand dollars in cash and a gold badge proclaiming the holder to be the High Sheriff of Suffolk County, Massachusetts.

The New York police called the Boston Police and described the man they had in custody: mid-40's, five feet, four inches tall, a hundred and seventy pounds, with a nasty scar running down the side of his face. Drunk as a skunk.

"That's our Johnny!" the Boston Police told their counterparts, and what's more, we've got a warrant for his arrest. Could the NYPD please get him cleaned up and hold him so he can be brought back to Boston to face charges?

The New York cops decided that they better get Johnny to a hospital to get his head stitched up and get him sober enough for the trip back to Boston. They brought him to Bellevue Hospital and he was admitted at 5:00 AM on Sunday the 12th.

As his head began to clear, Johnny realized he was in a world of trouble. He told detectives who were interviewing him that he had won the cash in his pocket from a lucky streak at the Narragansett Race Track in Pawtucket, Rhode Island, and asked to use a phone to call his wife.

A mad scramble ensued, as Boston Police, investigators from the District Attorney's office, the Boston news media and Johnny's wife and her brother all set off from Boston for Bellevue Hospital at breakneck speed.

Johnny Dowd had been living on his wits since his days back in Roxbury selling bogus raffle tickets, and he began to plot his escape. He befriended a hospital orderly and told him he was on his way to Los Angeles, but there had been a slight misunderstanding. Could the orderly possibly help claim

his money from the room where patient's valuables were stored and help him arrange alternative transportation? Johnny promised to make it worth the chap's efforts.

By the time Mary Dowd and her brother reached the hospital, a gaggle of Boston reporters and photographers were lining the sidewalk outside the hospital's main entrance, waiting to get a shot of Johnny being led out in handcuffs. The Boston Police and representatives from the DA's office were inside the hospital huddling with New York City Police and hospital security, planning on how to affect the arrest.

Mary Dowd and her brother helped Johnny into his street clothes. Mary was beside herself with worry that things would go wrong, but Johnny assured her that he had everything under control. He dispatched his brother-in-law to move the car around to the emergency fire exit, open the doors, and keep the motor running.

As the police delegation made its way up the front stairs to take Johnny into custody, the slippery sheriff was hobbling down the back stairs to the emergency exit a couple of thousand dollars poorer than when he checked in, but still a free man.

Reporters heard doors slamming and tires screeching, but by the time they rounded the building, all they caught was a glimpse of Johnny waving to them from the back seat of a late model sedan.

Johnny Dowd was in the wind.

THE MANHUNT

Efforts by law enforcement to find Johnny Dowd closely resembled a Keystone Kops comedy.

Initial reports had the outlaw sheriff being sighted in places as disparate as Philadelphia, Chicago, Florida, or hiding back in Boston. The Boston Police formed a Dowd Task Force and began staking out the homes of Johnny's relatives in Roxbury and Dorchester, and in the nearby towns of Weymouth and Milton.

A week after Johnny disappeared, his wife's uncle Ambrose was caught trying to cash a $4,000 check from Johnny at the First National Bank of Boston. Uncle Ambrose said Johnny had been in Boston over the weekend and had given him the check, and would contact him later to tell him where to send the money. Investigators from the DA's office grilled Ambrose to no avail. Employees at the bank told them Sheriff Dowd did indeed have a safe deposit box there. He had upgraded from a standard box to their largest model just after becoming sheriff, all the better to hold his ill-gotten loot.

A warrant was obtained to open the box, and a drill and an acetylene torch had to be used because Johnny's key was nowhere to be found. Inside the box was $48,000 cash, and the serial numbers and marks on the bills matched the list some of the Charles Street Jail guards had given Ruben Lurie of the bills they had paid Johnny to keep their jobs.

Meanwhile, tips continued to pour in about the whereabouts of Johnny Dowd, who was under a 32 count indictment that carried a possible jail sentence of up to 176 years. Four days after he was last seen in New York, he was reported sited in New Haven, Connecticut. The following day he was possibly spotted in Florida.

Six days into the manhunt, police were dispatched to check out sightings in Boston, Florida (again), and Mexico.

At the one week mark, Boston Police thought they had a credible tip that Johnny was hiding at a house in Boston's South End. An overnight stakeout and a massive raid at dawn turned up sleepy and confused residents of a home who had no connection with Sheriff Dowd and didn't have a clue where he might be hiding.

Soon, police departments across Massachusetts were inundated with tips of Johnny Dowd sightings, particularly after patrons imbibed at Saturday afternoon football games. Local cops raced to residences in Brookline, Sharon, Cambridge, Lawrence and Falmouth, all to no avail. Boston Police responded to a call to Beacon Hill, mere blocks from the Charles Street Jail, where a man swore he had captured Johnny Dowd and had him in custody. Officers arriving at the scene found the man who had called them very drunk and holding a poor soul who looked nothing at all like Johnny Dowd captive at the point of a Civil War era sword.

While the manhunt continued, conditions at the jail and details of Johnny's financial empire began to emerge in the press. In Chicago, Easy Eddie O'Hare, one of Johnny's rental tenants at the jail, was shot to death by gunmen wielding machine guns as he drove his car down a busy street. Back in Boston, three men were identified as Johnny's bag men, the guys who physically collected the bribes from employees and vendors at the jail. Within two days they had all turned state's evidence and were testifying

against Johnny. One man told the newspapers: "I stuck my chin out for him, and he didn't even get me a lawyer."

Boston's City Auditor got a look at the books of the Charles Street Jail and reported that he found such unusual items as five cases of bonded rye whiskey, in pints, for $195.; two cases of Madeira brandy, also in pints, for $37.; and boxes and boxes of oranges at a dollar a dozen. Many of the other accoutrements necessary for Johnny's restaurant were also on the jail's books: expensive cheeses and steaks, cocktail tables, lamps and luxurious chairs.

The District Attorney asked three different banks to freeze accounts Johnny had with them, and another $50,000 was found in a safe deposit box in New York City. Investigators revealed that Johnny also maintained a stock brokerage account with Wainwright and Company, and never let his balance get below $10,000. Not bad for a public servant with an annual salary of $7,000., two homes, and all that cash in those bank accounts and safe deposit boxes.

By the time Johnny had been missing for a month, frustrated Boston Police called in the G-Men to help with the search. The United States Attorney claimed that Johnny was transporting stolen property across state lines, and that made him eligible for an FBI posse. The intrepid *federales* boldly predicted that his capture was imminent.

The FBI sent out wanted posters with all ten of Johnny's finger prints and a stone faced picture of the diminutive fugitive with the scar running down his face. They were circulated nation-wide. Airports, train stations and even steamship lines were alerted to be on the lookout for the man wanted on Arrest Warrant #6150. The Boston Police sent out wanted posters to 70,000 gas stations across the country.

One Boston newspaper ran a feature story theorizing that Johnny would soon turn himself in because he was either homesick or just plain bored.

In early December reports began trickling in again, this time from a much wider area. He was in Nova Scotia. No, make that Detroit. Or possibly Windsor, Ontario. A report from Mexico City caused the Boston Police to send a Detective Captain to the Mexican capital only to come back empty handed. Yet another sighting had him in a Honolulu hospital being treated for kidney trouble. He was said to be on a beach in South America or up in the Great White North braving a Canadian winter. FBI agents from the local field office, acting on a hot tip, arrived at a motel in Helena, Montana, moments after a man fitting Johnny's description had left with a woman who closely resembled Mary Dowd, Johnny's wife. The manager thought the young couple might be on their way to the West Coast.

The Suffolk County Grand Jury continued to hear testimony about the high-jinx at Johnny's jail, and upped the indictment to sixty counts.

The State Commissioner of Corrections finished his investigation of conditions at the jail, which he termed "shocking" in a two hundred page report. All of the employees that Johnny had brought into the jail were dismissed and replaced with real prison guards hired on the merits.

On Christmas Day, 1939, the telephone rang at the home a neighbor of Johnny's mother. Would the man be kind enough to go across the street and see if Johnny's aged mother could come to the phone? He did, and Johnny was able to pass Christmas greeting along to his poor suffering mother. When police heard about the call and tried to question Mrs. Dowd, she refused to talk to them.

The relatives of Johnny's wife Mary were missing her and Mary's mother made a public appeal that Johnny either turn himself in, or let her go so that she could return to her family in Boston. A week later, Mary Dowd arrived in Boston by train. She went immediately to her parent's home in Dorchester, and refused all attempts by police to get her to answer questions. Each time the cops came to her house she started crying hysterically, and refused to say a single word to them. She would soon slip out of town under the cover of darkness and rejoin her fugitive husband on the lam.

A year passed and the trail grew cold. There were no more visits home, and no calls to relatives the following Christmas. It was beginning to look like Johnny had beaten the odds.

CAPTURED

John and Mary Norton were living the good life in Ventura, California. The retired couple from Chicago resided in a rented bungalow two blocks from the Pacific Ocean. From their peaceful palm tree lined street you could see the verdant slopes of the Ventura Hills in one direction and the gentle lapping surf of Pierpont Bay in the other.

Their well furnished house had two bedrooms, a large living room with a fireplace, a kitchen with all the modern appliances and a formal dining room. Their flagstone patio provided a nice view of the ocean. They parked their two year old sedan in the driveway next to the house. It was a safe neighborhood, and a Ventura cop lived right next door.

When the landlady told Mr. Norton what the monthly rent would be, he scoffed that he had nothing but money, and attempted to peal two month's rent off a wad of bills from his pocket. Somewhat embarrassed that his roll came up short, he turned to his wife, who opened the coat of her prim business suit to reveal a bulging money belt, from which she withdrew the balance.

John Norton spent leisurely days studying the Racing Form and placing bets at the Ventura County Fairgrounds located less than two miles from

their home. Norton often bragged to his landlady about his winnings at the horse track and flashed a lot of cash, but she noticed that he bristled at paying for minor items, and had to be reminded again and again to pay the paperboy or the man who mowed their lawn or to contribute the expected amount to the local Community Chest. Mary Norton made friends with the neighbors and spent her afternoons shopping, laying on the beach reading romance novels, or listening to baseball games on the radio.

Mary Norton was a big baseball fan who spent hours studying the box scores in the daily newspaper, particularly those of her beloved New York Yankees. As the 1941 baseball season began to draw to a close it was becoming clear that the World Series that year would be a subway series between the Brooklyn Dodgers and her Bronx Bombers. Mary Norton begged her husband to go to New York to watch the series in person, but John, who disliked baseball, said he didn't want to travel. He surprised her at breakfast one morning with a plane ticket back east to New York, and a reservation for a nice hotel room. She would be traveling alone.

John Norton drove his wife south to the Los Angeles airport for her flight, kissed her goodbye and drove off. But rather than return home, he kept on driving up the California coast through Santa Barbara and on up to San Luis Obispo, where he rented a motel room. Free from his wife's watchful eye, John was able to do what he loved most: drink. And drink he did. He found an Irish pub downtown and became a fixture there from the moment it opened until they turned out the lights and locked the door for the night. Norton sang Irish ballads in his off key voice, bought drinks for almost everyone in the joint and told all sorts of fabulous tales about the gangsters back in Chicago. He convinced the bartender to sell him a pint of whiskey to take the edge off on the two mile drive back to his motel.

Meanwhile, back in Boston, the Boston Police finally gave up the chase and announced on September 24, 1941, that they were disbanding the task force assigned to hunt for Sheriff John Dowd. They had spent twenty two months and thousands of dollars and countless man hours, but they were no closer to capturing Johnny Dowd than they were the day he slipped out the back door of a New York City hospital.

That very night, a Wednesday, was a slow night at the Irish pub in San Luis Obispo, so the bartender closed up early and sent an inebriated John Norton on his way with his customary pint of whiskey wrapped in a brown paper bag.

Norton was weaving his way along the road, singing an Irish song and swigging from the pint when he saw flashing red lights in his rearview mirror and heard a police siren. He pulled to the side of the road and waited as the cops approached both sides of his car and flashed their lights in his bleary eyes. Moments later he was in handcuffs in the back of the patrol car, headed for the San Luis Obispo jail.

The cops emptied his pockets, took his fingerprints and tossed him in a cell to sober up. The next morning they gave the hung over prisoner a ride to the local courthouse where a judge charged him a $100. fine and set him free, never for a moment realizing that the man before him with the bloodshot eyes and two day stubble was, in fact, the very much wanted John F. Dowd, formerly the high sheriff of Suffolk County, Massachusetts.

Johnny Dowd had fooled them again. He lived right next door to a police officer in Ventura, he had been stopped for traffic violations on more than one occasion, and now he had even been arrested without being found out as a fugitive. He had it made. He was bulletproof.

The police had no choice but to let "Mr. Norton" go, but they were concerned that he still wasn't sober enough to drive safely. On the way back to the station to pick up his car an officer saw two uniformed soldiers from the nearby Camp Luis Obispo hitchhiking and stopped and asked if either of them had a driver's license. Assured that they both had the necessary license to drive, he asked them if they would mind driving "Mr. Norton" south, as far as his residence in Ventura. They were happy to oblige, and Johnny was happy for the company.

Johnny had one request of his two new traveling companions: could they please stop at the Irish pub on the way out of town so Johnny could get a bottle for the road, a bit of the hair of the dog that bit him to deal with his horrific hangover?

They did, and the happy trio began driving down the coast. When they reached Santa Barbara, Johnny insisted that they stop at a fancy nightclub, where drinks and dinner were on him. Nothing but top shelf booze and the finest steaks.

Johnny was keeping up his act as "John Norton from Chicago," and the young soldiers asked him if he had known the mobster Easy Eddie O'Hare, who had been gunned down gangland style. "Sure," Johnny told them, "we were pals. He even used to stay at my place!"

By the time they reached Ventura, Johnny was sloppy drunk. He asked the soldiers to stay at his house and continue their party through the weekend. The soldiers agreed to stay overnight, but told Johnny they would be on their way in the morning.

Just before sunrise, Johnny was awakened by a crashing sound and sat up in bed startled. When he got his bearings he figured the noise was from the soldiers and began to relax. Suddenly the door to his bedroom burst open and he was staring down the barrels of two shotguns pointed at his head. Deputy Sheriffs from Ventura County were at the other end of the guns and they announced that John Dowd was under arrest.

The police in San Luis Obispo had had a bad feeling about the cocky drunk from Ventura that they had released in the custody of two young soldiers. They ran his fingerprints against the wanted posters they had on file and came up with a match for John F. Dowd of Boston. A quick call to the Boston Police confirmed that Dowd was still wanted, and another call to the Ventura County Sheriff resulted in the deputies being dispatched to apprehend him at his residence.

Johnny Dowd's life on the lam came to an abrupt end because he had married a Yankees fan. The Bronx Bombers, much to Mary Dowd's delight, won the World Series in five games. It was too bad for Johnny's sake that he hadn't married a Red Sox fan: the Sox finished 17 games out of first place that year.

HOMECOMING

When word reached Boston of Johnny's capture, three Boston Police detectives, including Lieutenant John J. Walkins, who had been assigned to the Dowd task force since day one, boarded a plane to Los Angeles to return their prized fugitive.

Johnny, for his part, was putting up a brave front, puffing on his ever-present cigar, and schooling the keeper of the Ventura County Jail on the finer points of running a lockup.

When the Boston cops arrived Johnny greeted them warmly, asked about their trip across the country, and encouraged them to see some of the California sights before they headed back.

He was being held on $50,000 bail as a fugitive from justice, but immediately waived any claim against extradition, telling his captors that he was "going home to face the music."

Johnny taunted the detectives who had failed to track him down for nearly two years, teasing them about some of the reports he'd read in newspapers while on the lam. "I got a kick out of reading about the manhunt, the places they say I've been,' Johnny said. "One day I heard I was

47

in Albany, New York, and that a detective had gotten my fingerprints off a glass there. That's pure bunk brother, I've never been in Albany, New York in my life!"

Always the sporting sort, Johnny bet the Boston detectives a box of cigars that the DA would never be able to make the charges stick. "It'll feel pretty tough though," Johnny mussed, "when I'm brought into Suffolk Superior Court. All I can think of is the swell job I had there as sheriff."

The following day, Johnny and the three detectives began their 3,200 mile trip back to Boston aboard a Union Pacific train. There was such a crush of media and security on the platform in Los Angeles that folks boarding the train assumed they were in the presence of some reclusive Hollywood star. That suspicion was only deepened when the train made a whistle stop in Cheyenne, Wyoming. Authorities had intercepted a postcard to Johnny from his wife postmarked Cheyenne, and carefully surrounded him as he stretched his legs, guarding against any sort of ambush that could free their prisoner.

The next stop was Chicago, where Johnny was booked into the jail at Police Headquarters for the night. Perhaps in return for the hospitality Johnny had shown Chicago mobsters when he rented them space at the Charles Street Jail, Johnny was treated like visiting royalty at the jail. He was assigned a comfortable cell, and provided with a delicious hot breakfast the following morning. He told the Boston detectives that the Chicago Police sure knew how to treat a guy, and proclaimed that he felt "fit as a fiddle." To top things off, a Captain of the Chicago Police took Johnny and the three Boston cops out to lunch at a fancy downtown restaurant before dropping them off at the train station for the rest of the journey home.

As the miles between Chicago and Boston clicked off, Johnny began to realize the seriousness of the situation. He would soon be standing before a judge who would hold him accountable for his outrageous behavior. Suddenly quiet and morose, Johnny meekly asked if he could be taken to a hospital rather than to a jail cell when they reached Boston. The request was denied, and when the train pulled into South Station, Johnny was handcuffed, brought before a judge for arraignment, and then loaded into the very Black Maria that had delivered prisoners to his jail back in the day.

The ride from Pemberton Square to the Charles Street Jail was a short one, perhaps a quarter mile. But the difference from how Johnny had last entered the building, as the proud proprietor, and now, as a manacled prisoner in denim garb was monumental. The Charles Street Jail was no longer the swank hotel for criminals that Johnny had created. Gone were the golf trips, gone were the fine dining and the wine cellar. The jail had reverted to being just a jail, and no one cared about the lack of female companionship for inmates, their laundry needs, or bar service straight to the cells. The Charles Street Jail was back to the routine of housing pre-trial detainees and prisoners.

If you're lucky enough to stay there today while visiting Boston, your experience will be much the same as when Johnny ran the place. Gone are the jail cell doors, the drab isolation unit and the steely eyed guards. You can get a drink delivered to your room, or you can dine in the fine restaurant known as the Clink. A cab to Cambridge for a round of golf at Fresh Pond awaits you at the curb, and you can arrange to have your laundry washed and folded and returned to your room.

During your visit you might walk the same path taken by the robbers from the Brinks Job, or duck out the same portal through which Trigger Burke escaped in a hail of bullets in 1954. Enjoy your stay in this historic masterpiece, but please take a moment to think of the outrageous story of Sheriff Johnny Dowd, a man ahead of his time.

re his face nor censure him too lavishly behind his back.—Francis Quarles.

Boston Post

2 CENTS

THURSDAY, SEPTEMBER 25, 1941 **   *Established 1831*   TWENTY-FOUR PAGES—TWO CENTS

DOWD TELLS HOW HE LIVED SINCE ESCAPE

Worked Three Days a Week Picking Apples, Lemons, Walnuts----Got $2.40 Per Day----Declares He's "Broke, Clean as Whistle"----Denies Wife With Him on Any Part of Flight----Crippled Now by Arthritis----Knew Arrest Certain

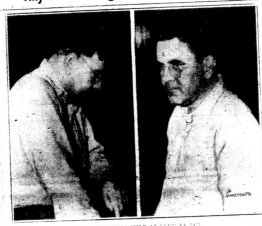

EX-SHERIFF DOWD HELD AT VENTURA JAIL

Leaving Boston Mistake----Took Poor Advice----Glad It's Over ----Ready to "Face Music"

Waives Extradition----May Reach Hub Monday to Face Court---- Held in $50,000 Bail

Here is former Sheriff John F. Dowd's own story, as given by telephone last night from the jail in Ventura, Calif., to John S. Mannion of the Boston Post.

BOY KILLED BY FALLING OUT OF TREE

Even after his capture, Johnny found it impossible to tell the truth.

Boston Globe editorial cartoon from September 25, 1941. Courtesy of the Globe Archives

Luxury Lockup Sources:

"The Purple Shamrock," by Joseph F. Dineen, (W.W. Norton & Co., 1949)
Pg 259-262; Pg264-269; Pg 273-274

"Fateful Rendezvous: The Life of Butch O'Hare," by Steve Ewing and John B. Lundstrom, (Naval Institute Press, 1997)
Pg 28; Pg 30-38; Pg 76-86

"Great Buildings of Boston, a Photographic Guide, by George M. Cushing, (Courier Dover Publications, 1982) Pg 42

Inmates of Charles Street Jail v. Eisenstadt, 360 F. Supplement 677 (District of Massachusetts, 1973)

Liberty Hotel website (www.libertyhotel.com/history) retrieved 4/21/2015

1926:

The Boston Globe:

"Fin Com Probes $225,463 Deal," 4/27/26 pg1
"Nichols Sends Man to 'Take The Rap,'" 6/8/26 pg1
"Favors $500,000 Snow-Removal Loan," 6/19/26 pg20
"Dowling Talks to District Attorney," 8/24/26 pg A1
"District Attorney Quizzes Bottomley," 8/24/26 pg4
"Councilors Dispute Over Polling Hours," 10/5/26 pg5
"Councilors Throw Out Dowd Note To Mayor," 10/19/26 pg2

1927:

The Boston Globe:

"Democrats Unite And Remove Keene," 1/11/27, pg1
"Council President Deadlock Continues," 1/18/27, pg28
"Heffernan Chosen Council President," 1/25/27, pg1
"Dowd Charges Innes and Others Run City," 3/29/27 pg7

1929:

The Boston Globe:

"Fuchs Declares Lynch Asked 13 $5000 Bribes," 1/3/29 pg1
"Councilors Named Deny All Charges," 1/3/29 pg23
"Guest of Fuchs Heard Judge Say 'Shakedown,'" 1/4/29 pg1
"Councilor Dowd to Wed June 17," 5/26/29 pgA16
"Ashmont Girl to Wed Councilor Dowd," 6/6/29 pg3
"Councilor Dowd to Marry June 17," 6/8/29 pg12
"Weather," 6/17/29 pg1
"City Councilor Dowd Weds Miss Margaret O'Connell," 6/18/29 pg13

1932:

The Boston Globe:

"Dowd A Candidate For Suffolk County Sheriff," 2/16/32 pg15
"Dowd Attributes High Tax Rate To Curley," 9/10/32 pg12
"Dowd Says Keliher Has Ignored Jail Economies," 9/18/32 pg43
"Weather," 9/13/32 pg1
"'Hecklers' Cause Fight At Rally," 9/13/32 pg12
"Dowd Gives Highlights Of His Council Career," 9/19/32 Pg12
"Keliher, Prendible In Van From Start," 9/21/32 pg1
"Barry Presses Swift To Finish," 9/22/32 pg1

1937:

The Boston Globe:

"Court Orders Quinn's Arrest," 2/26/37 pg1
"Former City Treas Dolan Indicted by Grand Jury," 10/17/37 pgA1

1938:

The Boston Globe:

"Yacht of E.L. Dolan Brings $10,500 at Auction in Quincy," 1/30/38 pgB25
"Dowd Asks $12,000 Contract Canceled," 5/8/38 pg12
"Charge Fixing in Dolan Case," 4/21/38 pg1
"Dowd Enters Race For Suffolk Sheriff," 6/11/38 pg12
"City Democratic League Backs Dowd For Sheriff," 6/13/38 pg9
"Curley Lashes Hurley, Kelly," 9/13/38 p6
"Weather," 9/21/38 pg2
"Sheriff Keliher Dead," 9/21/38 pg1
"Death Darkens Dowd Rejoicing," 9/21/38 pg14
"Sheriff Keliher Funeral Saturday," 9/22/38 pg2
"Suffolk County Sheriffs Long Termers," 9/25/38 pgB45
"Hurley Names Dowd Sheriff," 10/6/38 pg13
1938 (Continued)

"Sheriff Dowd Will Retain Assistants," 10/14/38 pg5
"Recount Requested On Cab Stand Issue," 11/13/38 pgC20
"Sheriff Dowd Takes Over New Courthouse, Escorts Mayor," 12/17/38 pg17
"Dowd to Open Court in Costume of 1775," 12/31/38 pg3

The New York Times:

"John A. Keliher," 9/22/38 pg23

The Boston Post:

"Sheriff Keliher Dies on Learning of Defeat-Dowd and Foley Both are Winners," pg1

1939

The Boston Globe

"1500 at Dinner Hear Sheriff Dowd Promise a Humane Administration," 1/26/39 pg13
"Costs at Sheriff's Residence $6,000," 1/13/39 pg9
"10 In Race For Dowd's Seat," 2/13/39 pg16

1939 (Continued)

"$2000 Pay Raise Voted for Dowd," 4/4/39 pg2

"Sheriff Dowd Asks Increased Budget," 4/6/39 pg3

"Six Relinquish Jobs at Suffolk Courthouse," 5/30/39 pg24

"Sheriff Submits Steprate Raises For Court Group," 7/1/39 pg8

"Sheriff to Dismiss 10 Courthouse Workers," 8/1/39 pg4

"Dowd Charges 'Frameup' in Inquiry by Boston Bar," 9/23/39 pg1

"Boston Bar Asks Sheriff Dowd Ouster," 9/29/39 pg1

"Sheriff's Request for Suspension of Employee Ignored," 9/30/39 pg16

"Remove Sheriff Dowd, Bar Asks," 10/4/39 pg1

"Dowd Says He'll Fight to Finish on Removal," 10/5/39 pg9

"Dowd Hearing Starts Today," 10/10/39 pg7

"Supreme Court Hearing Nov.13 in Dowd Ouster," 10/11/39 pg2

"Bar Extends Dowd Probe to Business," 10/20/39 pg1

"More Specifications Asked by Dowd," 10/21/39 pg16

"Juggins to Argue Plea for Dowd Tomorrow," 10/25/39 pg4

"Claims Discharge by Sheriff Drove Employee Insane," 10/27/39 pg13

"Further Answers to Dowd Refused," 10/28/39 pg16

"Federal Tax Men Will Attend Hearing," 11/1/39 pg14

"Resignation Talk 'Rumor,' Dowd Says," 11/2/39 pg12

"Sheriff First Witness in Ouster Proceedings," 11/3/39 pg5

"Workers Say Sheriff Dowd About to Quit," 11/7/39 pg1

"Dowd Leaves New York After Mysterious Mishap," 11/12/39 pgB1

"Saltonstall to Receive Dowd Resignation Today," 11/13/39 pg1

"$60,000 'Shakedown' Charged," 11/14/39 pg1

"Says Dowd Got Cash For Jobs," 11/15/39 pg1

"Foley Moves To Indict Today," 11/16/39 pg1

"$48,000 Sought In Dowd Case," 11/17/39 pg1

"Doyle Warns Name-Caller-Scrubwomen Shaken Down," 11/18/39 pg1

"Dowd Reported in Many Places," 11/18/39 pg3

"Seek to Indict Others in Dowd Probe," 11/19/39 pgB1

"Army Of Officials Look To Sheriff For Orders," 11/19/39 pgC9

"Foley Orders Dowd's Arrest," 11/21/39 pg1

"Foley Seeks to Open Box, Add Charges," 11/22/39 pg1

"Dowd Believed on Way to Coast," 11/23/39 pg1

"Dowd, If Convicted, Could Get 5 ½ Years Each on 32 Counts," 11/23/39 pg10

"Scrubwomen Say They Bought Jobs," 11/24/39 pg1

"Foley Is Told She Dunned Scrubwomen For Dowd Ring," 11/25/39 pg1

"To Ask Dowd Indictment for Taking Fees," 11/26/39 pgB1

"False Leads Harry Police in Dowd Hunt," 11/27/39 pg1

1939 (Continued)

"City Holds Up Bill for Water Coolers Ordered by Dowd," 11/28/39 pg10

"G-Men Called Into Hunt for Dowd," 11/28/39 pg3

"Police Look for Dowd in New York," 11/29/39 pg12

"Hussey Guarded After Threats in Dowd Case," 11/30/39 pg1

"Dowd Reported Seen in Detroit; Hunt Shifted," 12/1/39 pg22

"Sullivan May Put End to Deputy Sheriff Pool," 12/2/39 pg1

"Foley to Give Connolly Data to Grand Jury," 12/5/39 pg1

"67 Percent Profit Made on Coolers Sold to Dowd," 12/6/39 pg15

"Sheer Boredom Captures Many Clever Fugitives," 12/10/39 pgC2

"Selling Jobs Old Story Here, Says Farnum," 12/11/39 pg8

"Dowd Circulars Include but One of 60 Counts," 12/12/39 pg10

"Jail Officers Said Food Bad Under Dowd," 12/14/39 pg8

"Forgrave Was Jail 'Bookie,' Probers Say," 12/15/39 pg1

"Jail Cornerstone Word Misspelled," 12/17/39 pgC16

"Ex-Sheriff Dowd and Wife Traced to Helena, Mont.," 12/20/39 pg5

"Dowd Phoned Family Here on Christmas," 12/29/39 pg1

"Mother-in-Law Urges Ex-Sheriff Dowd's Surrender," 12/30/39 pg1

Boston Herald:

"Bar Charges Dowd With Extortion," 10/4/39 pg1

"Orders Dowd Arrest," 11/21/39 pg1

Boston Post:

"Summons Dowd Into High Court," 10/4/39 pg1

"Big Figure Involved In Dowd Case," 10/5/39 pg1

"Sheriff Dowd On Way Home," 11/12/39 pg1

"Foley Orders Dowd's Arrest," 11/21/39 pg1

The New York Times:

"Sheriff of Boston 16 Hours In Bellevue," 11/12/39 pg14

"Ex-Sheriff Is Reindicted," 11/24/39 pg42

"Fail to Find Indicted Ex-Sheriff," 11/26/39 pg28

1939 (Continued)

The Christian Science Monitor:

"Witnesses Tell Of Jail Favors In Dowd Probe," 11/14/39 pg11
"Jail Conditions Held Shocking," 12/11/39 pg11

Pittsburgh Post-Gazette

"Fugitive Sheriff's Auto Confiscated," 11/24/39 pg12

1940

The Boston Globe

"Wife of Ex-Sheriff Dowd Back, Mum as to Husband," 1/2/40 pg1
"Lyman Asks Jail Staff Slash," 1/19/40 pg1
"Fin Com Asks Duties at Jail Be Clarified," 2/12/40 pg16

Boston Post

"40 Dowd Aides to Lose Jobs at Jail," 1/19/40 pg1

Boston Herald

"Lyman Bares Jail Abuses," 1/19/40 pg1

The Christian Science Monitor

"Clearing the Atmosphere," 4/17/10 pg22

1941

The Boston Globe

"Dowd's Wife Reported at Parent's Home," 9/25/41 pg16

1941 (Continued)

"Broke, Picked Oranges, Dowd Says in Interview," 9/25/41 pg1

"Editorial Cartoon," 9/25/41 pg10

"Ex-Political Foe to Defend Dowd," 9/25/41 pg10

"$2500 Dowd Reward Likely to Go to West Coast Deputy," 9/25/41 pg1

"Dowd Faces Quiz by Federal Agents," 9/25/41 pg10

"'Anxious to Face Music,' Says Fugitive," 10/25/41 pg1

"Dowd is Held in $50,000 Bail," 9/25/41 pg1

"Dowd Co-Defendants in Jail, Case of Three Others Pending," 9/25/41 pg11

"Ex-Sheriff Dowd Says He Never Asked or Got Cash for Jobs," 9/26/41 pg1

"Dowd Denies Bribe Charges," 9/26/41 pg1

"Dowd's 76 Appointees May Testify if He Goes Before Jury," 9/26/41 pg16

"Dowd, Glum, Hits at 'False Friends' on Way to Boston," 9/27/41 pg1

"Dowd Too Ill for Trial, He Says, Will Ask Delay," 9/28/41 pg1

"Why Dowd Escaped Capture So Long," 9/28/41 pgC58

"Dowd Telegraphs Ex-Rep White to Act as Counsel," 9/29/41 pg4

"Dowd Arrives Here Today to Face Court," 9/30/41 pg1

"Ex-Sheriff Dowd in Dedham Jail; Trial Date Oct. 20," 10/1/41 pg1

"Dowd's Wife Pays Surprise Visit to Jail," 10/2/41 pg19

"Two Psychiatrists Named to Examine Ex-Sheriff Dowd," 10/3/41 pg12

"Ex-Sheriff Dowd Will Be Brought Into Court Today," 10/17/41 pg1

"Dowd Gets 6-8 Years, Enters State Prison," 10/18/41 pg1

The Christian Science Monitor

"Dowd Circulars Issued," 2/28/41 pg9

Boston Post

"Dowd Tells How He Lived Since Escape," 9/28/41 pg1

Boston Herald

"Dowd Starts Trip Home," 9/26/41 pg1

"Meteoric Career of Dowd Like Arabian Nights Chapter," 9/25/41 pg2

"Dowd's Mother Hires Counsel; Certain Her Son is Innocent," 9/25/41 pg2

"Dowd Ready to 'Face Music;' Fugitive Says 'It Doesn't Pay,'" 9/25/41 pg2

"Dowd Angry at Friends Who Deserted Him," 9/27/41 pg1

1941 (Continued)

"Dowd to Sleep in 3D Jail of Trip Tonight," 9/27/41 pg4
"Dowd Asks Hospital Care," 9/28/41 pg1

The New York Times

"Ex-Sheriff Dowd Pleads Guilty," 10/18/41 pg10

Other sources:

The Boston Globe

"FBI Nabs 'Trigger' Burke on Anniversary of Escape," 8/28/55 pgC1
"Added Guns, Men Guard Brink's Eight," 10/8/56 pg1
"Ex-Sheriff Dowd, 65, Dies in Hub Hospital," 8/16/61 pg25
"Ex-Sheriff Dowd's Personal Estate Worth $17,000," 11/24/62 pg17
"Two Boston Sheriffs Indicted in 22 Years," 5/26/61 pg20
"Many Defeats in Store, Lurie Tells Reformers," 5/15/53 pg14
"Louis Ladetto Seeks New Trial," 4/11/67 pg42

Boston Herald

"John F. Dowd Rites Friday," 8/15/63 pg10

Made in United States
North Haven, CT
11 November 2021